SECOND EDITION

TOUCHSTONE

WORKBOOK 1A

MICHAEL MCCARTHY

JEANNE MCCARTEN

HELEN SANDIFORD

CAMBRIDGE
UNIVERSITY PRESS

CAMBRIDGE
UNIVERSITY PRESS

University Printing House, Cambridge CB2 8BS, United Kingdom

One Liberty Plaza, 20th Floor, New York, NY 10006, USA

477 Williamstown Road, Port Melbourne, VIC 3207, Australia

314–321, 3rd Floor, Plot 3, Splendor Forum, Jasola District Centre, New Delhi – 110025, India

79 Anson Road, #06–04/06, Singapore 079906

Cambridge University Press is part of the University of Cambridge.

It furthers the University's mission by disseminating knowledge in the pursuit of education, learning and research at the highest international levels of excellence.

www.cambridge.org
Information on this title: www.cambridge.org/9781107670716

First published 2005
Second Edition 2014

20 19 18 17 16 15 14 13 12 11 10 9 8 7 6 5 4 3 2

Printed in the United Kingdom by Latimer Trend

A catalog record for this publication is available from the British Library.

ISBN 978-1-107-67987-0 Student's Book
ISBN 978-1-107-62792-5 Student's Book A
ISBN 978-1-107-65345-0 Student's Book B
ISBN 978-1-107-63933-1 Workbook
ISBN 978-1-107-67071-6 Workbook A
ISBN 978-1-107-69125-4 Workbook B
ISBN 978-1-107-68330-3 Full Contact
ISBN 978-1-107-66769-3 Full Contact A
ISBN 978-1-107-61366-9 Full Contact B
ISBN 978-1-107-64223-2 Teacher's Edition with Assessment Audio CD/CD-ROM
ISBN 978-1-107-61414-7 Class Audio CDs (4)

Additional resources for this publication at www.cambridge.org/touchstone2

Contents

1 Meetings and greetings

Vocabulary | **A** Complete the conversations. Choose and write the best response.

1. A Hello.

    B _Hi._

    a. Hi.

    b. Good-bye.

2. A Hi. I'm Ted.

    B _____

    a. Hi, I'm Lucille. Nice to meet you.

    b. See you next week.

3. A How are you?

    B _____

    a. I'm Kyle.

    b. I'm fine, thanks.

4. A Good-bye.

    B _____

    a. See you later.

    b. Thanks.

5. A Good night.

    B _____

    a. Hello.

    b. Bye. See you tomorrow.

6. A Hi. How are you?

    B _____

    a. Good, thanks. How are you?

    b. Have a nice day.

Vocabulary | **B** Complete the conversations with the expressions in the box.

Good night.	✓Hello.	How are you?	Nice to meet you.
Have a good evening.	Hi.	I'm fine	See you

1. Jack _Hello._ I'm Jack.

   Anna _____ I'm Anna.

   Jack _____

2. Sonia Hi, Julie. How are you?

   Julie Good. _____

   Sonia _____ , thanks.

3. Mike _____

   Koji Thanks. You too.

4. Joan _____

   Mary Bye. _____ tomorrow.

C Complete the instant message.

Instant Message	▭ ◻ ✕
Sandra	Good morning, Jenny.
Jenny	_Good morning_ , Sandra.
Sandra	_____ are you?
Jenny	_____ , thanks. _____
Sandra	Good.
Jenny	See you later.
Sandra	OK. _____ a nice day.
Jenny	Thanks. _____ too.
Sandra	Bye.

3

1 My name's Eva.

Vocabulary | Complete the conversation.

A Good morning.

B Good morning.

A How are you?

B I'm fine.

A What's your __name__?

B Eva Salazar.

A How do you spell your _____ name?

B It's S-A-L-A-Z-A-R.

A And what's your _____ name?

B Eva.

A OK. How do you _____ *Eva*?

B E-V-A.

A And are you Ms., Miss, or _____ ?

B Ms.

A Thank you. Have a nice day.

B Thanks. You too.

2 Your personal information

Vocabulary | Complete the form. Use your own information.

Touchstone English Club

NAME: _____

              First   Middle   Last

☐ single   ☐ married

CLASS: _____

ROOM: _____

TEACHER: _____

3 Are we in the same class?

Grammar **A** Complete the conversation. Write *am* or *are*. Use contractions *'m* or *'re* where possible.

Receptionist Hello. ___Are___ you here for
an English class?

Mi-Young Yes, I _____ . I'm Mi-Young.

Receptionist Mi-Young Lee? You _____ in Class C.

Mi-Young Thank you.

Sergio Hi. _____ I in Class C, too? I'm Sergio.

Receptionist Yes, you _____ .

Sergio So we _____ in the same class.

Receptionist Wait. _____ you Sergio Rodrigues?

Sergio No, I _____ not. I'm Sergio Lopes.

Receptionist Oh, you _____ in Class D.
You _____ not in the same class.

B Complete the conversation.

David Hi. _____ _____ Julia Kim?

Leti No, _____ _____ . I'm Leticia Martinez,
but everyone calls me Leti.

David Hi, Leti. I'm David. Nice to meet you.

Leti _____ _____ here for a dance class?

David Yes, _____ _____ . _____ _____
in the same class?

Leti Yes, _____ _____ . We're in Class A.

4 About you

Grammar Answer the questions. Use your own information.

1. Are you in an English class?

   _____

2. Are you in a French class?

   _____

3. How are you today?

   _____

4. Are you and your friends in the same English class?

   _____

5. Are you married?

   _____

1 What's the number?

Vocabulary **A Write the numbers.**

0	1	2	3	4	5
zero	_____	_____	_____	_____	_____

6	7	8	9	10
_____	_____	_____	_____	_____

B Complete the crossword puzzle.

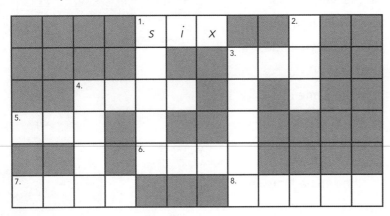

Across

1. two × three = ____six____

3. two + eight = _____

4. ten ÷ two = _____

5. six – four = _____

6. three + six = _____

7. five × zero = _____

8. six + two = _____

Down

1. ten – three = _____

2. eight – seven = _____

3. eight – five = _____

4. two × two = _____

2 What's the word?

Vocabulary **The letters spell a word. Write each letter in the correct box below to see the word.**

1. C	3. H	5. N	7. E	9. U
2. O	4. O	6. T	8. S	10. T

ten	four	nine	one	three	eight	six	two	five	seven
			C						

3 Here's your membership card.

Grammar | Look at Mark's student ID card. Write his answers in the conversation.

Lee Hello. Are you a member of the club?

Mark No, I'm not.

Lee OK. Well, here's an application form. So, what's your last name?

Mark *It's Brokaw.* or *Brokaw.*
or *My last name's Brokaw.*

Lee Thank you. And your first name?

Mark _____

Lee What's your middle initial, please?

Mark _____

Lee And what's your email address?

Mark _____

Lee And your phone number?

Mark _____

Lee Are you an English student?

Mark _____

Lee What's your teacher's name?

Mark _____

Lee Thank you. Here's your membership card. Have a nice day.

Student ID Card
Mark A. Brokaw

Telephone: 740-555-2968
Email: mab@cup.org
Department: English (Mrs. Roberts)

4 About you

Grammar and vocabulary | Write questions with *What's* and the words given. Then answer the questions with your own information.

1. A *What's your name?*
        (your name)

   B _____

2. A _____
        (your cell phone number)

   B _____

3. A _____
        (your email address)

   B _____

4. A _____
        (your English teacher's name)

   B _____

1 Good evening.

Complete the conversations with the expressions in the box. Use each expression only one time.

Good evening.	✓ Hi	How about you?	How are you doing?	Thank you.	Yes
Pretty good.	Hello.	Nice to meet you.	Good-bye.	thanks.	Yeah

1. Sam   Hi, Ali.

   Ali   ___*Hi*___ , Sam. _____

   Sam   Good, thanks. How about you?

   Ali   _____

   Sam   Am I late?

   Ali   _____ , you are, but it's OK.

   Sam   Good. By the way, here's your book.

   Ali   Oh, _____

2. Joe   Good evening.

   Clerk _____ What's your name, please?

   Joe   Joe Johnson.

   Clerk Oh, yes. Mr. Johnson. Your room number is

           10A. Here's your key.

   Joe   _____

3. Sally Hello. My name's Sally.

   Kate   _____ I'm Kate. _____

         Are you here on business?

   Sally _____ , I am. _____

   Kate   No, I'm on vacation.

   Sally Nice. Oh, here's a taxi. _____

   Kate   Bye.

② How are you doing?

A Rewrite the conversation. Use less formal expressions for the underlined words.

A <u>Hello. How are you?</u>   A *Hi. How are you doing?*

B <u>I'm fine, thank you.</u> How are you?   B _____

A <u>I'm fine.</u> Are you a student here? A _____

B <u>Yes,</u> I am. How about you?   B _____

A <u>Yes,</u> me too.   A _____

B What's the email address here?

A It's goodschool1@cup.org.

B <u>Thank you. Good-bye.</u>   B _____

A <u>Good-bye.</u>   A _____

B Number the lines of the conversation in the correct order. Then write the conversation.

____ Hi.   A *Hello.* _____

____ Yeah, me too.   B _____

____ OK.   A _____

____ Are you here for the concert?   B _____

____ How are you doing?   A _____

_1_ Hello.   B _____

____ Yeah, I am. How about you?   A _____

Unit 1 Progress chart

What can you do? Mark the boxes. ✔ = I can . . . ? = I need to review how to . . .	To review, go back to these pages in the Student's Book.
☐ make statements with *I'm (not)*, *you're (not)*, and *we're (not)*.	2, 4, and 5
☐ ask questions with *Are you . . . ?*	5
☐ ask questions with *What's . . . ?*	4, 6, and 7
☐ give answers with *It's . . . .*	6 and 7
☐ say *hello* and *good-bye* in at least 4 different ways.	1, 2, and 3
☐ talk about names in English.	2 and 4
☐ use numbers 0–10.	6
☐ use *How about you?*	8
☐ use everyday expressions in more formal and less formal situations.	9

Grammar / Vocabulary / Conversation strategies

1 Where is everybody today?

Grammar | **A** Look at the pictures. Complete the sentences.

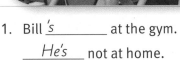

1. Bill _'s_____ at the gym.
   __He's___ not at home.

2. Jon and Karen ____are____ at home. _____ not in class.

3. Sun-Yee _____ in the cafeteria. _____ late.

4. David _____ on vacation. _____ asleep.

5. Kate and Tess _____ in class. _____ not at the library.

6. Carmen _____ at work. _____ not sick.

B Complete the questions about the people in part A. Then answer the questions.

1. A ____Is____ Bill at work?
   B _No, he's not._____

2. A _____ Jon and Karen at home?
   B _____

3. A _____ Sun-Yee at the gym?
   B _____

4. A _____ David asleep?
   B _____

5. A _____ Kate and Tess on vacation?
   B _____

6. A _____ Carmen at work?
   B _____

2 Absent classmates

Grammar | Complete the conversation with the verb *be*. Use contractions where possible.
Add *not* where necessary.

Silvia   Hi. How ____*are*____ you?

Jason   Good, thanks. How about you?

Silvia   Pretty good. _____ Dave here?

Jason   No, he _____ _____ .
I think he _____ sick.

Silvia   Oh. _____ he at home?

Jason   I don't know.

Silvia   How about Jenny and Paula?
_____ they here?

Jason   No, they _____ _____ . They _____
on vacation. I think they _____ in Miami.

Silvia   Look! Dave _____ not sick. He _____ over
there. He _____ just late again!

3 About you

Grammar and vocabulary | Complete the questions with the names of your friends and classmates.
Then answer the questions.

1. A Is ____*Paul*____ at home?
   B ____*Yes, he is.*_____

2. A Are _____ and _____ at work?
   B _____

3. A Is _____ in class today?
   B _____

4. A Are _____ and _____ on vacation?
   B _____

5. A Are _____ and _____ in your English class?
   B _____

6. A Is _____ sick today?
   B _____

7. A Is _____ at the library?
   B _____

8. A Are _____ and _____ asleep?
   B _____

1 Everyday things

Vocabulary | Label the things in the pictures. Use *a* or *an* where necessary.

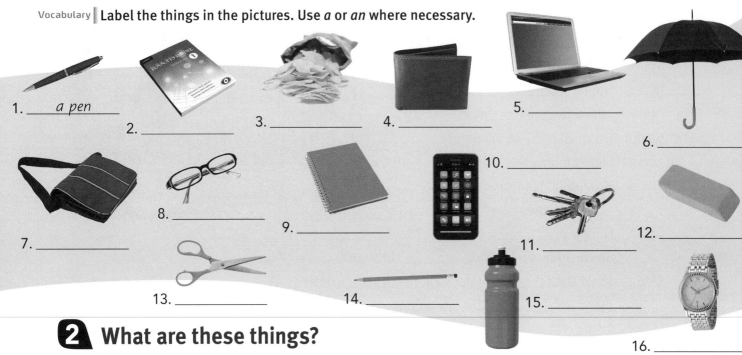

1. _____a pen_____

2. _____

3. _____

4. _____

5. _____

6. _____

7. _____

8. _____

9. _____

10. _____

11. _____

12. _____

13. _____

14. _____

15. _____

16. _____

2 What are these things?

Grammar and vocabulary | Write sentences about the pictures.

1. _This is a bag._

2. _These are pens._

3. _____

4. _____

5. _____

6. _____

7. _____

8. _____

3 Asking about things

| **Complete the conversations. Use the words in the box.**

Is	it	it's	these	they're	this	What
Is	it's	these	they	they're	this	✓What's

1.
Clerk	You're in Room 102.
Ms. Simms	Thanks. _What's_ this?
Clerk	Oh, _____ your room key.
Ms. Simms	OK. Thank you.
Clerk	And _____ is your membership card for the fitness club.

2.
Erica	What's _____ ? _____ it a smartphone?
Jim	No, _____ not. It's a GPS.
Erica	Oh.
Jim	_____ are these?
Erica	I think _____ watches.

3.
Bob	What are _____ ?
Jill	Oh, no! I think _____ my jeans.
Bob	Oh, I'm sorry. Are _____ new?
Jill	Yeah. Oh, look. _____ this your wallet?
Bob	Yes, _____ is.
Jill	Oh, no! And _____ are your credit cards!

1 Classroom things

Vocabulary | **A** Write the words under the pictures. Use *a* or *some*.

1. _a board_
2. _some posters_
3. _____
4. _____

5. _____
6. _____
7. _____
8. _____

9. _____
10. _____
11. _____
12. _____

B Circle the words from part A in the puzzle. Look in these directions (→ ↓). Which word is *not* in the puzzle?

T	V	C	Q	U	A	B	L	A	M	A	B
W	E	H	A	S	I	P	U	Y	A	Z	O
A	C	A	L	E	N	D	A	R	P	H	A
G	O	I	H	K	O	B	Z	O	E	O	R
I	P	R	P	E	D	L	F	L	T	E	D
W	A	S	T	E	B	A	S	K	E	T	I
R	K	T	O	R	R	J	O	O	M	U	M
O	C	U	O	S	J	E	C	D	E	S	K
N	L	L	G	T	O	R	X	I	T	J	A
C	O	M	P	U	T	E	R	O	T	D	S
M	C	A	S	M	P	O	S	T	E	R	S
A	K	S	C	I	S	S	O	R	S	A	R

2 A classroom

Grammar
and
vocabulary **A** Look at the picture. Complete the sentences. Use the words in the box.

in	in front of	in front of	next to	✓on	on	on	under

1. The workbooks are ___on___ the table.
2. The calendar is _____ the wastebasket.
3. The computer is _____ the teacher's desk.
4. The map is _____ the window.

5. The students' papers are _____ the wall.
6. The teacher's desk is _____ the board.
7. The scissors are _____ the teacher's desk.
8. The table is _____ the chairs.

B Write the questions about the classroom in part A.

1. A _Where's the teacher's desk?_
   B It's in front of the board.

2. A _____
   B It's next to the window.

3. A _____
   B They're on the table.

4. A _____
   B They're under the teacher's desk.

5. A _____
   B They're on the wall.

6. A _____
   B It's in the wastebasket.

3 Missing apostrophes

Grammar | Put apostrophes (') in the correct places in the questions. Then answer the questions.

1. What's on the wall in your classroom? _____

2. What are your friends names? _____

3. Whats your English teachers name? _____

4. Wheres your teacher now? _____

1 Questions, questions

Conversation strategies Complete the conversations. Use the expressions in the box.

✓Excuse me	Thanks anyway.	Sure.	Here you go.	Thanks.
Can I borrow	You're welcome.	please	How do you spell	Sorry.
What's the word for this in English?				

1. Callie   _Excuse me_ , Bob.

   Bob   Yeah?

   Callie   _____ your English book?

   Bob   Sure. Now, where is it?

   Callie   Um . . . it's right in front of you.

   Bob   Oh, yeah. _____

   Callie   Thanks.

   Bob   _____

2. Ruby   Can I borrow your cell phone,

   _____ ?

   Millie   _____ Oh, wait.

   It's not in my bag. I think it's at home.

   _____

   Ruby   That's OK. _____

   Millie   Sure. . . . _____

   Ruby   In English, the word is *umbrella*.

   Millie   Umbrella? Thanks.

   Ruby   Sure.

3. Yuri   _____ *computers*?

   Dan   C-O-M-P-U-T-E-R-S.

   Yuri   _____

   Dan   Sure.

   Yuri   And how do you spell *television*?

   Dan   T-V.

   Yuri   Very funny!

2 Scrambled conversations

Conversation strategies **Number the lines of the conversations in the correct order. Then write the conversations.**

1. _____ I'm sorry.   A *You're late.* _____
   ___1___ You're late.   B _____
   _____ That's OK.   A _____

2. _____ Sure.   A _____
   _____ Thank you.   B _____
   _____ Can I borrow your pen, please?   A _____
   _____ You're welcome.   B _____

3. _____ I don't know.   A _____
   _____ That's OK. Thanks anyway.   B _____
   _____ That's OK. What about this?   A _____
   _____ I'm sorry. I don't know.   B _____
   _____ What's the word for this?   A _____

Unit 2 Progress chart

What can you do? Mark the boxes. ✓ = I can . . . ? = I need to review how to . . .	To review, go back to these pages in the Student's Book.
☐ make statements with *he's (not)*, *she's (not)*, and *they're (not)*.	12 and 13
☐ ask questions with *Is he . . . ?*, *Is she . . . ?*, and *Are they . . . ?*	13
☐ use *a* or *an*.	14
☐ make nouns plural with *-s*, *-es*, or *-ies*.	15
☐ use *this* with singular nouns and *these* with plural nouns.	14 and 15
☐ ask questions with *Where . . . ?*	17
☐ use *'s* and *s'* to show possession.	17
☐ name at least 8 things students take to class.	14 and 15
☐ name at least 12 classroom items.	16 and 17
☐ say where things are in the classroom.	16 and 17
☐ ask for help in class.	18
☐ use common responses to *Thank you* and *I'm sorry*.	19

Grammar

Vocabulary

Conversation strategies

1 Favorites

Vocabulary | **A** Unscramble the letters. Write the words.

1. rgiens   s _inger_

2. ctrao   a_____

3. rtweir   w_____

4. maet   t_____

5. ralype   p_____

6. dnab   b_____

7. prsot   s_____

8. naf   f_____

9. ivome   m_____

10. rtiats   a_____

B Complete the crossword puzzle with the words in part A.

Across

3. Adele is an amazing _____ .

5. Our favorite soccer _____ is Manchester United.

8. Hugh Jackman is a great _____ .

10. Ronaldo is a famous soccer _____ .

Down

1. Soccer is a _____ .

2. J.K. Rowling is a famous _____ .

4. Who's your favorite _____ ?

6. This _____ is exciting.

7. My favorite _____ is Coldplay.

9. Brian is a _____ of the Giants.

2 She's my favorite singer.

Grammar | **Look at the pictures. Complete the sentences.**

1. " _She's_ my favorite singer.
   Her new album is great."

2. "_____ Jama fans. Jama is
   _____ favorite band."

3. "_____ a great writer.
   _____ new book is really
   good."

4. "_____ favorite movie is
   The Aliens. What's _____
   favorite movie?"

5. "_____ my favorite actors.
   I think _____ movies are
   very good."

6. "Cassandra Coe is my teacher.
   _____ a great artist. _____
   pictures are amazing."

3 They're great!

Grammar | **Complete the conversation with the verb *be*. Use contractions where possible.**

Alicia   I love this new Bruno Mars album. He _'s_ my favorite singer.

Norah   Yeah. I _____ a big fan of his, too. His voice _____
        amazing. His songs _____ great.

Alicia   Yeah. So, what's your favorite band?

Norah   Maroon 5. They _____ great.

Alicia   Yes, they _____ very talented. Adam Levine _____ really
        good looking. He _____ my favorite.

1 What are they like?

Vocabulary | Look at the pictures. Complete the sentences. Use the words in the box.

| busy | fun | lazy | ✓quiet | smart | tired |
| friendly | interesting | outgoing | shy | strict | |

1. She's _____quiet_____ and _____ .

2. He's _____ .

3. They're _____ .

4. She's _____ .

5. She's _____ .

6. He's _____ .

7. He's not very _____ or _____ .

8. They're _____ . She's _____ .

2 What's new?

Grammar | Complete the conversation with the verb *be*. Use contractions where possible.
Add *not* where necessary.

Carrie Sorry. ___Am___ I late?

Josh No, you _____ _____ . You _____ fine.

Carrie Good. So, what's new? _____ you busy at work?

Josh Yes, I _____ . Our boss _____ sick,

so he _____ _____ at work.

Carrie Oh, really?

Josh So, how about you? What _____ your new

neighbors like? _____ they nice?

Carrie Yes, they _____ . They _____ OK.

They _____ very quiet.

Josh _____ they students?

Carrie No, they _____ _____ . The guy _____ a writer.

Josh A writer? What about the woman? _____ she a writer, too?

Carrie No, she _____ _____ . She _____ _____ a writer – she _____ a teacher. At our school!

3 Make it negative.

Grammar | Rewrite the sentences in the negative form. Use contractions where possible.

1. My neighbors are very nice.   *My neighbors aren't very nice.* _____

2. My best friend is a student.   _____

3. I'm very shy.   _____

4. The students in my class are very smart. _____

5. My English class is easy.   _____

6. My teacher is very quiet.   _____

4 About you

Grammar and vocabulary | Complete the questions. Then write short answers. Add more information.

1. ___Are___ you outgoing?   *Yes, I am. I'm very outgoing.* _____

   or   *No, I'm not. I'm not outgoing.* _____

2. _____ your best friend lazy?   _____

3. _____ your English class hard? _____

4. _____ your friends smart?   _____

5. _____ your teacher fun?   _____

6. _____ your classmates nice?   _____

7. _____ you tired today?   _____

8. _____ you and your friends busy after class? _____

1 Who's who?

Vocabulary | Use the family tree to complete the sentences about this family.

1. David is Paul's ___son___ .
2. John is Katy's _____ .
3. Katy is Paul's _____ .
4. Josh, David, and Emily are Paul and
   Katy's _____ .
5. Emily is Josh's _____ .
6. Josh is David's _____ .
7. John and Catherine are
   Katy's _____ .
8. Katy is Josh's _____ .
9. John is Catherine's _____ .
10. Emily is Katy's _____ .
11. Catherine is David's _____ .
12. John is Emily's _____ .
13. Susan is David's _____ .
14. Bill is Josh's _____ .
15. Robert is Emily's _____ .

2 What's the number?

Vocabulary | Write the numbers.

65

1. ___sixty-five___

11

2. _____

24

3. _____

15

4. _____

16

5. _____

91

6. _____

56

7. _____

77

8. _____

3 How about your children?

 Complete the conversations. Write the full questions.

1. A How / your parents?

   How are your parents?

   B They're fine. Thanks. How / your mom?

   _____

   A She's good. She's on vacation right now.

2. A What / your sisters' names?

   _____

   B Beth and Kate. My brother's name is Pete.
   A Pete? Oh, how old / he?

   _____

   B He's 21.

3. A Who / this?

   _____

   B Oh, it's my aunt.

4. A My cousins are really fun.
   B Yeah? How old / they?

   _____

   A They're my age.

5. A Where / your family today?

   _____

   B At home. How about your family?
   A They're at home, too.

6. A Where / you from?

   _____

   B Well, my parents are from Italy originally.
   A Really? Where / your parents from in Italy?

   _____

   B They're from Rome.

4 A famous family

Grammar | **Read part of a phone interview with an actor. Then write questions for the answers.**

Interviewer   Hello, Kate. How are you?

Kate   Hi. I'm fine, thanks.

Interviewer   Kate, I love your movies.

Kate   Thank you.

Interviewer   Now, about your family . . . who's your mother?

Kate   Gwen Russell – the artist. And Kevin Russell is my father.

Interviewer   Yes, they're famous! What are your parents like at home?

Kate   Oh, Dad's fun and outgoing. And Mom's very smart!

Interviewer   And, Kate, what's your favorite band?

Kate   Imagine Dragons. They're amazing. . . .

1. *How is Kate?*

   She's fine.

2. _____

   Her mother is Gwen Russell.

3. _____

   Her father is fun and outgoing. Her mother is very smart.

4. _____

   Her favorite band is Imagine Dragons.

1 New neighbors and co-workers

Conversation strategies | Complete the conversations with the questions in the box.

How old is she?	Where is she from?	✓What are they like?	An actor? Is she good?
From Chile?	Are they friendly?	Are they good?	Where are they from?

1. Ming   Who are they?

   Jim   Oh, they're my new neighbors.

   Ming   Your neighbors? *What are they like?*

   Jim   Interesting. Very interesting. They're in a
          rock band.

   Ming   A rock band? _____

   Jim   They're from New York.

   Ming   Wow! _____

   Jim   No, they're not.

   Ming   Uh-oh. _____

   Jim   Oh, very. Their friends are always here!

2. Carlos   Who's she?

   Kim   Her name's Angie.

   Carlos   Angie? _____

   Kim   I don't know exactly. I think she's from Chile.

   Carlos   _____ Really?

          What's she like?

   Kim   She's outgoing and fun.

   Carlos   Really? _____

   Kim   I'm not sure. Maybe 24 or 25.

   Carlos   Oh. What's her job? Is she a server here?

   Kim   Well, yes. But she's an actor, too.

   Carlos   _____

   Kim   Yeah, she's a good actor but not a great server.

2 Really? I'm surprised!

Write responses to show you are interested or surprised. Then ask a question.

1. My grandmother's name is Banu.   _Really? What's she like?_

2. My brother is a singer in a band.   _____

3. My grandfather is a tennis player.   _____

4. I'm from Alaska.   _____

5. My mother is a Spanish teacher.   _____

6. My new job is hard work.   _____

7. My sister is an artist.   _____

8. My last name is Oh.   _____

Unit 3 Progress chart

What can you do? Mark the boxes. ✓ = I can . . . ? = I need to review how to . . .	To review, go back to these pages in the Student's Book.
Grammar	
☐ use *my*, *your*, *his*, *her*, *our*, and *their*.	22 and 23
☐ make statements with *be*.	22 and 23
☐ ask *yes-no* questions with *be*.	24 and 25
☐ make negative statements with *be*.	24 and 25
☐ ask information questions with *be*.	26 and 27
Vocabulary	
☐ name at least 8 words to describe people's personalities.	24 and 25
☐ name at least 12 family words.	26 and 27
☐ say numbers 10–101.	26
Conversation strategies	
☐ show interest by repeating information and asking questions.	28
☐ use *Really?* to show interest or surprise.	29

1 What's Kathy's morning like?

 Grammar and vocabulary

A Complete the sentences about Kathy's morning. Use the correct form of the verbs in the box.

check	exercise	✓ get up	play
eat	get up	listen	read

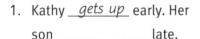

1. Kathy __*gets up*__ early. Her son _____ late.

2. She _____ before work. Her son _____ games.

3. She _____ to the radio in the car.

4. She and her co-workers _____ breakfast together.

5. Kathy _____ her email right after breakfast.

6. Her boss _____ the newspaper at work.

B Rewrite the sentences in the negative form. Use contractions where possible.

1. Kathy's son gets up early. __*Kathy's son doesn't get up early.*__

2. Kathy checks her email before breakfast. _____

3. Kathy and her son talk a lot in the morning. _____

4. Kathy's son does his homework. _____

5. Kathy and her boss eat breakfast together. _____

6. Kathy's boss plays computer games. _____

2 Guess what!

Grammar | Complete Peter's email with the correct form of the verbs.

New Message   ⊟ ⬜ ✕

To: Samir22@cup.com
From: PeterJ@cup.com
Subject: New Job   🔍

Hi!

Guess what! I ___*have*___ (have) a new job – in a coffee shop. It's hard work. I _____ (get up) early, and I _____ (work) late. But the coffee is good.

My boss is nice. He's French, and he _____ (study) English at night. He _____ (do) his homework in the coffee shop. I _____ (help) him sometimes. He's quiet, and he _____ (not / talk) a lot. He _____ (listen) to the radio and _____ (sing), but we _____ (not / like) the same music. He _____ (like) coffee, too. We both _____ (have) four cups of coffee every day!

Write soon!

Peter

---

3 Typical morning activities

Grammar and vocabulary | **A** What are typical morning activities? Match the verbs with the words and expressions.

1. do ___*d*___
2. study _____
3. check _____
4. listen _____
5. drive _____
6. play _____
7. read _____
8. go _____

a. to the radio
b. (my) email or messages
c. a car
✓d. (my) homework
e. on the Internet
f. English
g. games on the computer
h. a book

B Write true sentences about your morning routine. Use the verbs in part A.

1. *I don't do my homework in the morning.* _____
2. _____
3. _____
4. _____
5. _____
6. _____
7. _____
8. _____

1 What's fun? What's not?

Vocabulary **A** Which routine activities are fun for you? Complete the charts. Add your own ideas.

check email	do the laundry	go shopping	take a class
clean the house	eat snacks	make phone calls	text friends
do homework	get up early	✓ play sports	watch TV

Fun!	
play sports	

Not fun!	

B Write the days of the week in the date book. Then write one thing you do each day.

S *unday*   : *I go shopping on Sundays.*   **Th**_____ : _____

M_____ : _____   **F**_____ : _____

T_____ : _____   **S**_____ : _____

W_____ : _____

2 About you 1

Grammar and vocabulary
Use time expressions to write one thing you do and one thing you don't do.

1. on the weekends   *I clean the house on the weekends.*

   I don't go to work on the weekends.

2. after work / class   _____

   _____

3. every day   _____

   _____

4. on Saturdays   _____

   _____

5. in the afternoons _____

   _____

6. at night   _____

   _____

3 What's your week like?

Grammar | **Complete the conversation with the correct form of the verbs.**

Cecilia What's your week like, Eduardo? ___Do___
(Do / Does)

you ___go___ to work every day?
(go / goes)

Eduardo Well, no, I _____ . I work at home on Fridays.
(don't / doesn't)

Cecilia Really? What about on the weekends? _____
(Do / Does)

you _____ then, too?
(work / works)

Eduardo Yes, I _____ . But I don't like it. What
(do / does)

about you? _____ you and your husband
(Do / Does)

_____ to work every day?
(go / goes)

Cecilia Yes, we _____ . But just Monday to Friday.
(do / does)

We _____ the house on the weekends.
(clean / cleans)

Oh, and we _____ to soccer games.
(go / goes)

Eduardo Oh. _____ your son _____ soccer?
(Do / Does)   (play / plays)

Cecilia Yes, he _____ . He's on the school team.
(do / does)

_____ your son _____ any sports?
(Do / Does)   (play / plays)

Eduardo No, he_____ . He plays games on his computer.
(don't / doesn't)

4 About you 2

Grammar and vocabulary | **Complete the questions. Then write answers with your own information.**

1. A ___Do___ you ___take___ a class at night?
   B _Yes, I do. I take a Spanish class on Monday evenings._

2. A _____ your father _____ the laundry on weekends?
   B _____

3. A _____ you and your friends _____ shopping on Saturdays?
   B _____

4. A _____ your friends _____ their email before breakfast?
   B _____

5. A _____ your mother _____ the news on the Internet every day?
   B _____

1 Saying more than *yes* or *no*

Conversation strategies

A Complete the conversation. Use the sentences in the box.

I work part-time in the cafeteria.	It's fun, and the people are nice.
Just Mondays and Wednesdays.	I'm an English student.
✓ I'm new here, and I'm late.	I go there Mondays after work. It's great!

Mike   Hi. Are you OK? You look lost.

Yumi   Hello. Where's Room 106? Do you know?
I'm new here, and I'm late.

Mike   Yeah. It's right over there, next to the cafeteria.

Yumi   Thanks. So, do you work here?

Mike   Yes, I do. _____

Yumi   Do you like the job?

Mike   Yeah, I do. _____

Yumi   That's good. Do you work here every day?

Mike   Well, no. _____
I go to class on Tuesdays and Thursdays.

Yumi   Oh. So you're a student, too?

Mike   Yeah. _____

Yumi   Really? I'm an English student, too. Do you belong
to the English Club?

Mike   Yes, I do. _____

Yumi   Oh. Well, thanks a lot. And see you at English Club!

Mike   Great!

B Read the completed conversation again. Then read the sentences below.
Check (✓) *T* (true) or *F* (false).

	T	F
1. Mike and Yumi are friends.	☐	✓
2. Mike works in the cafeteria.	☐	☐
3. Mike is a new student.	☐	☐
4. Mike works Tuesdays and Thursdays.	☐	☐
5. Mike likes his part-time job.	☐	☐
6. Yumi and Mike are English students.	☐	☐
7. Mike belongs to the English Club.	☐	☐

2 About you

Conversation strategies **Unscramble the questions. Then answer the questions. Write more than *yes* or *no*. Use *Well* if you need to.**

1. live / you / around / Do / here ?

   Do you live around here?

2. from / originally / you / here / Are ?

3. a / full-time / you / Are / student ?

4. have / you / brothers / Do / sisters / or ?

5. you / work / the / on / weekends / Do ?

6. Do / your / every day / text / friends / you ?

7. get up / day / you / Do / every / early ?

8. grandparents / Do / with / your / live / you ?

1 Watching TV

Reading **A** What do you think average Americans do after work and school?
Check (✓) three boxes.

☐ spend time with family   ☐ read   ☐ watch TV
☐ go out with friends   ☐ go out to dinner   ☐ go shopping

B Read the article. Check your answers in part A.

After WORK and SCHOOL

Do Americans go out every night after work and have fun? Maybe the answer is surprising, but no, they don't. They don't usually go out with friends in the evening, and they don't go out to dinner or go shopping. So what do they do? Well, about 90% of Americans stay at home in the evening to relax. In fact, it's their favorite activity. They read, watch TV, and spend time with their families.

So what about young people? Well, they spend a lot of time at home, too. American high school students study about six hours a week and watch TV for about 15 hours a week.

Most Americans also have a hobby and do fun, interesting things like play sports or music. Americans stay home a lot, but they stay busy, too!

Here are average Americans' favorite activities:

• reading
• watching TV
• spending time with their families
• exercising
• using the Internet

TV Set

C Read the article again. Then correct these false sentences.

1. Americans go out with friends every night after work.
   Americans don't usually go out with friends in the evening.

2. After work, Americans usually go shopping.
   _____

3. American high school students usually study for three hours a night.
   _____

4. American high school students don't watch TV.
   _____

5. The average American doesn't have a hobby.
   _____

2 Weekends

Writing **A** Read the email messages. Then rewrite Joe's message. Use capital letters and periods.

Hi Joe,
Are you busy on weekends?
I am. On Friday nights, I go to a club in Miami. On Saturdays, I sleep late. In the evening, I watch TV. On Sundays, I study. Do you study on the weekends?
Ian

hi ian,
yes, i have busy weekends on friday nights, i visit my family downtown on saturdays, i take a spanish class at grove college on sundays, i play soccer i don't study on weekends – i don't have time
joe

Hi Ian,
_____
_____
_____
_____
_____
_____
_____

B What do you do on weekends? Write an email to a friend about your weekend activities.

New Message

Hi _____ ,
_____
_____
_____
_____
_____
_____

Unit 4 Progress chart

What can you do? Mark the boxes. ✔ = I can . . . ? = I need to review how to . . .	To review, go back to these pages in the Student's Book.
Grammar ☐ make simple present statements.	34 and 35
☐ ask simple present *yes-no* questions and give short answers.	36 and 37
Vocabulary ☐ name at least 12 new verbs for routine activities.	34, 35, 36, and 37
☐ name the days of the week.	36
☐ name at least 8 time expressions with the simple present.	37
Conversation strategies ☐ answer questions with more than *yes* or *no*.	38 and 39
☐ use *Well* to get time to think of an answer.	39
Writing ☐ use capital letters and periods.	41

Free time

Going out

1 In your free time

Vocabulary | How often do you do these things? Complete the chart with the free-time activities in the box.
Add your own ideas.

| ✓ eat out | go out with friends | go to a club | go to the gym | play a sport |
| go on the Internet | go shopping | go to a movie | have dinner with family | text family |

every day	three or four times a week	once or twice a week	once or twice a month
		eat out	

2 Craig's busy schedule

Grammar and vocabulary | **A** Read Craig's weekly planner. Are the sentences below true or false? Write *T* (true) or *F* (false).
Then correct the false sentences.

WEEKLY PLANNER

SUNDAY	MONDAY	TUESDAY	WEDNESDAY	THURSDAY	FRIDAY	SATURDAY
5	**6**	**7**	**8**	**9**	**10**	**11**
morning: *do the laundry!!*	morning: *classes*	morning: *go to the gym!*	morning: *classes*	morning: *go to the gym!*	morning: *classes*	morning: *clean the house!!*
	afternoon: *go shopping*	afternoon: *library*	afternoon: *guitar lesson*			afternoon: *tennis with Bob*
evening: *dinner with Mom and Dad*				evening: *dinner with Sandra*	evening: *movie with Jim*	evening: *club with Bill*

three evenings a week

1. He goes out with friends ~~every evening~~. *F*

2. He goes to the library every day. ____

3. He goes shopping once a week. ____

4. He takes guitar lessons on Wednesday

   mornings. ____

5. He plays tennis twice a week. ____

6. He does the laundry three times a week. ____

7. He sees his parents on the weekends. ____

8. He cleans the house on Saturday

   mornings. ____

Grammar | **B Now answer these questions about Craig's schedule.**

1. How often does he go to the gym?   *He goes to the gym twice a week.*
2. When does he have classes?   _____
3. How often does he go to a club?   _____
4. What does he do on Thursday evenings?   _____
5. When does he go to the movies?   _____
6. What does he do on Saturday afternoons?   _____
7. Who does he play tennis with?   _____
8. Where does he go on Saturday evenings?   _____

3 About you

Grammar and vocabulary | **Write questions for a friend. Then answer your friend's questions.**

1. You   *Where do you go after class?*
         (go after class)

    Friend   I meet some friends and go to a restaurant for dinner.
             How about you?

    You   _____

2. You   _____
         (text your friends)

    Friend   Every day. But I don't text before breakfast. How about you?

    You   _____

3. You   _____
         (do in your free time at home)

    Friend   I rent a movie, or I just relax in front of the TV with a friend.
             How about you?

    You   _____

4. You   _____
         (go on the weekends)

    Friend   I go to a restaurant or club. How about you?

    You   _____

5. You   _____
         (go out with)

    Friend   Oh, friends from school. How about you?

    You   _____

1 How often?

Grammar **A** Write the frequency adverbs in order in the chart below.

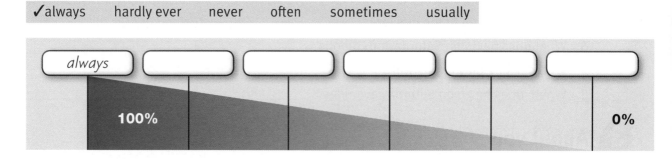

✓always   hardly ever   never   often   sometimes   usually

| always | | | | | |

100%   0%

B Answer the questions. Write true sentences using frequency adverbs.

What's something you . . .

1. hardly ever do before school or work?   *I hardly ever check my email before school.*
2. always do in the morning?   _____
3. sometimes do after school or work?   _____
4. never do during dinner?   _____
5. often do in the evening?   _____
6. usually do on Saturdays?   _____

2 What kinds of TV shows do you know?

Vocabulary **A** Look at the pictures. Circle the correct type of TV show.

1. (soap opera)/
   the news

2. talk show /
   cartoon

3. sitcom /
   the news

4. cartoon /
   game show

5. documentary /
   talk show

6. talk show /
   cartoon

7. sitcom /
   reality show

8. the news /
   game show

B Circle the kinds of TV shows from part A in the puzzle. Look in these directions (→↓).

T	C	S	I	T	C	O	M	E	T	I	S
E	A	O	E	D	H	P	O	R	H	I	H
L	R	E	A	L	I	T	Y	S	H	O	W
K	T	A	L	K	S	H	O	W	U	P	O
S	O	A	P	O	P	E	R	A	E	E	U
D	O	C	U	M	E	N	T	A	R	Y	N
A	N	O	O	T	H	E	J	E	I	W	S
Y	T	E	A	I	U	W	D	O	C	T	V
Y	C	G	A	M	E	S	H	O	W	L	Y

3 About you

Grammar
and
vocabulary

Answer the questions. Give two pieces of your own information in each answer.

1. Do you ever watch soap operas? *Yes, I usually watch soap operas in the afternoons.*
   I love the stories.

2. What sitcoms do you hardly ever watch? _____
   _____

3. How often do you watch documentaries? _____
   _____

4. What talk shows do you like? _____
   _____

5. When do you usually watch the news? _____
   _____

6. How often do you watch reality shows? _____
   _____

1 Asking questions in two ways

Conversation strategies Complete the conversations with the questions in the box.

Do you like French?	I mean, do you belong to any clubs?
✓ Do you do anything special?	I mean, do you know a nice place?
Do you play baseball?	I mean, do you go every day?

1. **Lisa** What do you do after work?
   Do you do anything special?

   Debbie Well, I go to the gym.

   Lisa Really? How often do you go?

   _____

   Debbie No, not every day. I go Mondays, Wednesdays, and Thursdays.

2. **Howard** Do you know the restaurants around here?

   _____

   Mary Well, I often go to a little place on Main Street. What kind of food do you like?

   _____

   Howard Yes, I do. I love French food.

3. **Paul** What do you do after school?

   _____

   Tom Well, yeah. I'm in the Sports Club.

   Paul Really? What do you play?

   _____

   Tom Well, no. We watch baseball on TV!

   Paul Oh.

2 Questions, questions

Conversation strategies | **Write a second question for each question below. Then write true answers.**

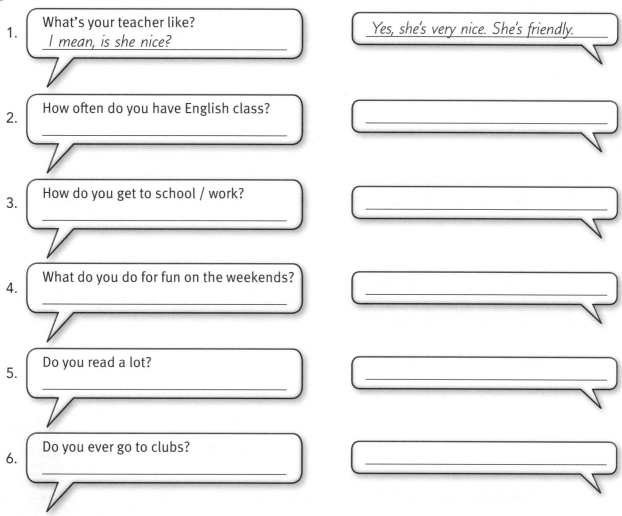

1. What's your teacher like?
   I mean, is she nice?

   Yes, she's very nice. She's friendly.

2. How often do you have English class?
   _____

   _____

3. How do you get to school / work?
   _____

   _____

4. What do you do for fun on the weekends?
   _____

   _____

5. Do you read a lot?
   _____

   _____

6. Do you ever go to clubs?
   _____

   _____

3 About you

Conversation strategies | **Add frequency adverbs to make these sentences true for you.**
Then use *I mean*, and write more information.

1. I ___never___ go to the gym. _I mean, I usually exercise at home._ _____

2. I _____ get home early. _____

3. I _____ see my friends during the week. _____

4. I _____ go on the Internet in the evening. _____

5. I _____ eat breakfast at school / work. _____

6. I _____ get up early. _____

7. I _____ eat out on Saturdays. _____

8. I _____ watch reality shows on TV. _____

9. I _____ go shopping on the weekends. _____

10. I _____ study English after dinner. _____

1 Paula's problem

Reading **A** Read Paula's post to an online forum. How many hours does Paula spend online?

☐ 3 or 4 hours   ☐ 4 or 5 hours   ☐ 8 or 9 hours

PaulaT18   posted 2 hours ago

I live with my parents and my two brothers. They say I hardly ever spend time with them. My parents say I spend too much time on my phone and in front of my computer, but I don't think that's true. I mean, I often get up early and check my messages, but we always eat breakfast together. I guess I sometimes text during breakfast, but I never call people then. After class, I listen to music on my phone, but I also do my homework. In the evening, I often log on to my social network to chat with friends. They're always online. Sometimes I watch a movie on my computer. I usually spend eight or nine hours online every day. I don't think it's a problem. What do you think?

B Read Paula's post again. Then answer the questions.

1. Who does Paula live with? _She lives with her parents and her two brothers._

2. Is she a student? _____

3. When does she log on to her social network? _____

4. What does Paula use her phone and computer for? _____

5. What do you think? Does Paula have a problem? Why or why not? _____

40

2 I need some advice!

Writing **A** Read José's post to an online forum. Complete it with *and* or *but*.

José posted 2 hours ago

I think I have a problem. I don't have a computer at home, ___*but*___ I use a computer at school. I usually go to school early, _____ I check my email. I send email to my friends in other countries. I often go online for fun, _____ sometimes I study English on the computer. Then on the weekends, I go to school _____ write papers for class (on the computer). Do I spend too much time at school?

B Write a post for an online forum about a problem you have. Write about a problem below, or use your own idea.

"I watch too much TV."   "I go shopping too much."   "I work too much."

"I stay home too much."   "I talk on my cell phone too much."   "I study too much."

Unit 5 Progress chart

What can you do? Mark the boxes. ✔ = I can . . . ? = I need to review how to . . .	To review, go back to these pages in the Student's Book.
Grammar	
ask simple present information questions.	44 and 45
use time expressions like *once a week*.	44 and 45
use frequency adverbs like *sometimes*, *never*, etc.	46
Vocabulary	
name at least 6 new free-time activities.	44 and 45
name at least 6 kinds of TV shows.	47
talk about likes and dislikes.	47
Conversation strategies	
ask questions in 2 ways to be less direct.	48
use *I mean* to repeat an idea and say more.	49
Writing	
use *and* and *but* to link ideas.	51

41

Neighborhoods

Lesson A / Nice places

1 What's in the neighborhood?

Vocabulary │ Label the places in the picture. Use the words in the box with *a / an* or *some*.

✓apartment buildings	fast-food places	museum	park	restaurants	supermarket
club	movie theater	outdoor café	post office	stores	swimming pool

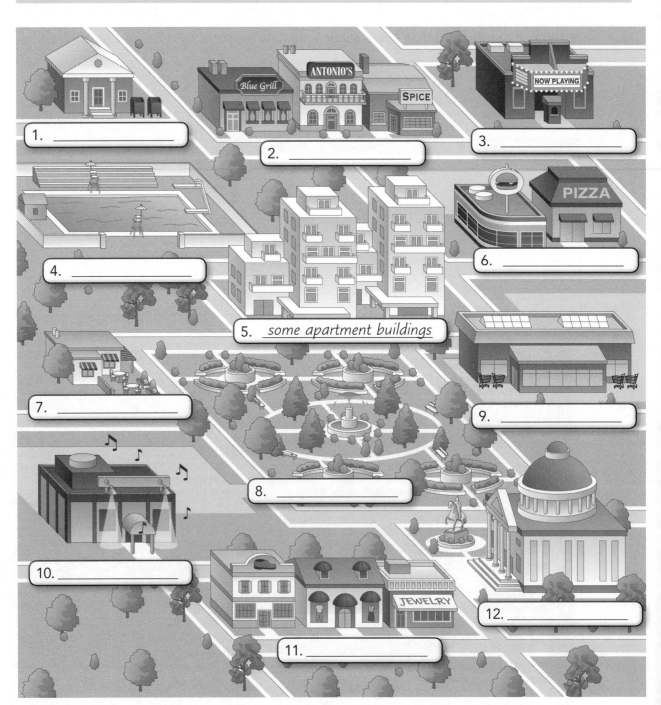

1. _____

2. _____

3. _____

4. _____

5. _some apartment buildings_

6. _____

7. _____

8. _____

9. _____

10. _____

11. _____

12. _____

2 Can you find the opposites?

Vocabulary | Find six pairs of adjective opposites in the box. Write them in the chart below.

bad	boring	expensive	interesting	noisy	quiet
big	cheap	good	✓new	✓old	small

new – old

3 That's not quite right!

Grammar | Look at the picture on page 42. Correct the sentences to describe the neighborhood.

1. There's one cheap fast-food place.   *There are a couple of cheap fast-food places.*
2. There are a couple of post offices.   _____
3. There's a big stadium.   _____
4. There are a couple of supermarkets.   _____
5. There are some malls.   _____
6. There's an apartment building.   _____
7. There are no small stores.   _____
8. There's an expensive restaurant.   _____
9. There are a lot of beautiful parks.   _____
10. There's no movie theater.   _____

4 About you

Grammar and vocabulary | What's your neighborhood like? Complete the sentences with true information.

1. There's a _____ .
2. There are a lot of _____ .
3. There are some _____ .
4. There are a couple of _____ .
5. There's no _____ .
6. There are no _____ .

43

1 What's the time?

Vocabulary **A** Write the times in words. Where there are two lines, write the times two ways.

1. *It's twelve p.m.*

   It's noon.

2. _____

   _____

3. _____

4. _____

5. _____

   _____

6. _____

   _____

B Read about Kayo's day. Write the times in numbers. Then number the sentences in the correct order.

_____ Her bus comes at ___*7:55*___ (five to eight).

_____ She gets home at _____ (nine fifteen) and watches TV.

___*1*___ Kayo gets up at _____ (six twenty-five).

_____ She goes for lunch with her co-workers at _____ (noon).

_____ She starts work at _____ (eight forty-five).

_____ She meets her boyfriend at _____ (twenty five to six), and they have dinner.

_____ She eats breakfast at _____ (twenty after seven).

_____ She leaves work at _____ (ten after five).

_____ She goes to bed at _____ (ten thirty).

2 Let's do it!

Grammar | Complete the conversations. Write questions starting with *What time . . . ?*
Use *Let's* to end each conversation with a suggestion.

1. A I'm starving. Let's go to Burger Queen.

   B But it's late. *What time does it close?*

   A It closes around 11:00, I think. _____

   B Almost 10:00. _____

2. A There's a new reality show on TV tonight.

   B _____

   A Um, I think it starts at 8:00.

   B Well, I'm really tired. _____

   A I'm not sure. I think it ends at 9:30.

   B OK. _____

3. A Let's go to the gym on Saturday morning.

   B Sure. _____

   A Oh, it opens early. At 6:00. _____

   B I usually get up around 8:00 on Saturdays.

   A OK. _____

3 About you

Grammar and vocabulary | Unscramble the questions. Then write true answers.

1. do / What time / get up / on weekdays / you ?

   A *What time do you get up on weekdays?*

   B _____

2. your family / have / What time / does / lunch / on Sundays ?

   A _____

   B _____

3. your English class / What time / start / does ?

   A _____

   B _____

4. What time / leave home / do / you / in the morning ?

   A _____

   B _____

5. stores / do / What time / in your neighborhood / open and close ?

   A _____

   B _____

1 Responses

Conversation strategies Circle the two correct responses to each comment. Cross out the incorrect response.

1. I think every neighborhood needs a park.
   a. ~~Me neither.~~
   b. (Me too.)
   c. (Right.)

2. We don't have a good fast-food place here.
   a. Yeah.
   b. Me too.
   c. I know.

3. I don't like the new restaurant.
   a. Yeah. I know.
   b. Me neither.
   c. Me too.

4. There are no good bookstores around here.
   a. I know.
   b. Me too.
   c. Right.

5. I like the new outdoor café downtown.
   a. Me neither.
   b. Me too.
   c. Right. It's good.

6. I love this neighborhood. It's so quiet.
   a. Right.
   b. Yeah, I know.
   c. Me neither.

2 What do they have in common?

Conversation strategies Read the conversation. Are the sentences below true or false? Write *T* (true) or *F* (false).

Glen What's your new neighborhood like?

Anna Oh, it's amazing. There are a lot of outdoor cafés and movie theaters and clubs. I go out a lot.

Glen Really? I hardly ever go out in my neighborhood. It's boring.

Anna Let's do something in my neighborhood this weekend. I'm free on Saturday.

Glen Me too.

Anna Well, there's a great jazz club near my apartment. I love jazz.

Glen Really? Me too!

Anna But let's have dinner at a café first. The food at the club is expensive, and I don't have a lot of money.

Glen Me neither. So, let's meet at 6:30 at your apartment.

1. Glen and Anna both like their neighborhoods. ___F___

2. Glen and Anna both go out a lot in their neighborhoods. _____

3. Glen and Anna are both free on Saturday. _____

4. Glen and Anna both love jazz. _____

5. Glen and Anna both have a lot of money. _____

> **✎ Help note**
>
> Glen and Anna **both** love jazz. Glen loves jazz, **and** Anna loves jazz, **too**.

3 Right. I know.

Conversation strategies | Circle the expression that is true about your neighborhood. Then show you agree. Respond with *Right* or *I know*.

1. A (There are some)/ **There are no** good restaurants in my neighborhood.
   B *I know.*

2. A My neighborhood **has** / **doesn't have** a lot of great stores.
   B _____

3. A I live in a **great** / **terrible** neighborhood.
   B _____

4. A We **need** / **don't need** a shopping mall around here.
   B _____

4 About you

Conversation strategies | Imagine you're talking to people from your neighborhood. Write true responses.

1. I really like this neighborhood.

   Me too. I think it's great.
   or
   Really? I don't like it very much.

2. I don't eat out in this neighborhood.

   _____
   _____

3. I think the restaurants are very expensive here.

   _____
   _____

4. I don't know a lot of people around here.

   _____
   _____

5. I think our neighborhood is boring.

   _____
   _____

6. I think we need a couple of new stores in our neighborhood.

   _____
   _____

1 Free weekend events!

Reading **A** Read about some local events on a website. Match the pictures with the events. Write the correct numbers next to the pictures.

○○○

Downtown Weekend Section

* * * FREE EVENTS * * *

1. All Day Music Meet local bands, singers, and musicians at City Park this Sunday. Listen to great music, dance to pop songs, or take a music workshop and write your own song! The music starts at 3 p.m. and finishes at 11 p.m. Call Melissa at 555-9075 for more information.

2. Spring Food Festival Do you love food? Do you often eat out? Then come to the Parkview Food Festival. Eat some delicious food from 20 different restaurants around the neighborhood – all for FREE!
Saturday from 11:00 a.m. to 4:00 p.m. at Green Street Park.

3. Outdoor Street Fair *Saturday and Sunday from 10:00 a.m. to 6:00 p.m. in front of the City Art Museum.* There are a lot of beautiful items for sale – books, art, photos, paintings, clothes, and more. Items for sale are just $2–$25. Coffee, sodas, and snacks are for sale, too!

4. Free Classes at the Neighborhood Center Do you want to take a class but don't have the time? Try a free one-hour class Monday through Friday this week. Learn:
- Art   • Spanish   • Music
- French   • Computers   • Yoga

Classes start at 10:00 a.m. and 2:00 p.m. Go to www.freeclass.cup.org for more information.

B Read the website again. Then answer the questions. Check (✓) the correct events.

Which events . . .	The concert	The food festival	The street fair	The free classes
1. have food?	☐	✓	✓	☐
2. are on Saturday?	☐	☐	☐	☐
3. have a website?	☐	☐	☐	☐
4. are during the day?	☐	☐	☐	☐
5. are at night?	☐	☐	☐	☐
6. are outdoors?	☐	☐	☐	☐

2 Make your own event.

Writing **A** Complete the sentences with the prepositions in the box.

| at | at | at | between | for | ✓from | on | through | to |

1. The event is __from__ 6:00 _____ 10:00.
2. The event is _____ 8:00 p.m. _____ the stadium _____ Main Street.
3. Go to www.eventinfo.cup.org _____ more information, or call Jim _____ 555-7777.
4. Call _____ 12:00 p.m. and 5:00 p.m., Monday _____ Friday.

B Imagine you are planning an event. Answer the questions. Use the ideas in the boxes and your own ideas.

Events:	Places:
a play, an art exhibit, a concert, a sports event	the library, the museum, the park, the theater

1. What is the event? _____
2. When and where is it? _____
3. What time does it start and finish? _____
4. What's the cost of the event? Is it free? _____
5. What things are there to do at the event? _____
6. Where or how do people get more information? _____

C Write an ad for an event in your town or city. Give the event a name.

_____

_____

_____

Unit 6 Progress chart

What can you do? Mark the boxes. ✓ = I can . . . ? = I need to review how to . . .	To review, go back to these pages in the Student's Book.
Grammar	
☐ use *There's* and *There are* with singular and plural nouns.	54 and 55
☐ use quantifiers *a lot of*, *some*, *a couple of*, and *no*.	54 and 55
☐ use adjectives before nouns.	55
☐ ask and answer questions about time.	56 and 57
☐ make suggestions with *Let's*.	57
Vocabulary	
☐ name at least 6 adjectives to describe places.	54 and 55
☐ name at least 10 words for neighborhood places.	54 and 55
☐ give times for events.	56 and 57
Conversation strategies	
☐ answer *Me too* or *Me neither* to show I'm like someone.	58 and 59
☐ answer *Right* or *I know* to agree.	59
Writing	
☐ use prepositions *at*, *from*, *in*, *on*, and *to* with times, places, and days.	61

Illustration credits

Ken Batelman: 42   **Harry Briggs:** 15, 61 *(4 at bottom)*, 69   **Domninic Bugatto:** 8, 23, 27, 38, 59, 78   **Cambridge University Press:** 67
Matt Collins: 22, 54   **Chuck Gonzales:** 5, 11, 26, 45, 80   **Cheryl Hoffman:** 3, 24, 47, 61 *(2 at top)*   **Jon Keegan:** 19, 51, 94, 95
Frank Montagna: 2, 13, 21, 53, 82, 83   **Greg White:** 7, 16, 37, 79   **Terry Wong:** 30, 46, 63, 74, 86   **Filip Yip:** 70

Photo credits

3 *(clockwise from top left)* ©Exactostock/SuperStock; ©Elea Dumas/Getty Images; ©MIXA/Getty Images; ©Thinkstock   **4** ©Ryan McVay/Getty Images   **7** ©wavebreakmedia/Shutterstock   **10** *(clockwise from top left)* ©Andresr/Shutterstock; ©MTPA Stock/Masterfile; ©Spencer Grant/PhotoEdit; ©Jose Luiz Pelaez Inc./Corbis; ©Medioimages/Photodisc/Thinkstock; ©Terry Doyle/Getty Images   **11** *(top to bottom)* ©Image Source/SuperStock; ©kurhan/Shutterstock   **12** *(pen)* ©Phant/Shutterstock; *(potato chips)* ©Thinkstock; *(wallet)* ©AlexTois/Shutterstock; *(laptop)* ©Alex Staroseltsev/Shutterstock; *(umbrella)* ©K. Miri Photography/Shutterstock; *(bag)* ©Hemera Technologies/Thinkstock; *(glasses)* ©Ingvar Bjork/Shutterstock; *(keys)* ©SELEZNEV VALERY/Shutterstock; *(notebook)* ©zirconicusso/Shutterstock; *(smartphone)* ©Oleksiy Mark/Shutterstock; *(water bottle)* ©lucadp/Shutterstock; *(eraser)* ©GreenStockCreative/Shutterstock; *(watch)* ©Venus Angel/Shutterstock; ©Butterfly Hunter/Shutterstock; *(pencil)* ©Julia Ivantsova/Shutterstock; *(hand holding smartphone)* ©Thinkstock; *(hand holding water bottle)* ©DenisNata/Shutterstock; *(all others)* ©George Kerrigan   **14** *(top row, left to right)* ©Rtimages/Shutterstock; ©Cambridge University Press; ©Thinkstock; ©Cambridge University Press *(middle row, left to right)* ©Ryan McVay/Thinkstock; ©Ryan McVay/Thinkstock; ©Thinkstock; ©Pixtal/age Fotostock *(bottom row, left to right)* ©Cambridge University Press; ©Cambridge University Press; ©Photodisc/Thinkstock; ©vovan/Shutterstock   **19** ©Design Pics/SuperStock   **20** *(clockwise from top left)* ©Exactostock/SuperStock; ©Exactostock/SuperStock; ©Mark Scott/Getty Images; ©Fancy Collection/SuperStock; ©Andreas Pollok/Getty Images; ©Ron Chapple/Getty Images; ©rSnapshotPhotos/Shutterstock; ©Peter Cade/Getty Images   **28** ©Don Nichols/Getty Images   **29** *(top to bottom)* ©Larry Dale Gordon/Getty Image; ©Punchstock   **32** *(television)* ©Maxx-Studio/Shutterstock   **35** *(top to bottom)* ©Darren Mower/Getty Images; ©Thinkstock   **36** *(top row, left to right)* ©JOSE LUIS SALMERON Notimex/Newscom; ©The Everett Collection; ©The Everett Collection; ©Getty Images *(bottom row, left to right)* ©Lions Gate/courtesy Everett Collection; ©Eric Roberts/Corbis; ©Robert Voets/CBS via Getty Images; ©Ann Johansson/Corbis   **40** ©violetblue/Shutterstock   **43** *(left to right)* ©Maxx-Studio/Shutterstock; ©MariusdeGraf/Shutterstock   **44** *(clockwise from top left)* ©Cambridge University Press; ©Artur Synenko/Shutterstock; ©Cambridge University Press; ©Cambridge University Press; ©Cambridge University Press; ©Cambridge University Press   **45** ©Punchstock   **47** ©Anders Blomqvist/Getty Images   **48** *(left to right)* ©Ambient Images Inc./Alamy; ©Yellow Dog Productions/Getty Images; ©Spencer Grant/PhotoEdit; ©David Grossman/Imageworks   **50** *(clockwise from top left)* ©Holly Harris/Getty Images; © Kwame Zikomo/SuperStock; © Jens Lucking/Getty Image; © Kaz Chiba/Getty Images; © Onoky/SuperStock; © I. Hatz/Masterfile   **52** *(top row, all photos)* ©Cambridge University Press *(middle row, left to right)* ©Cambridge University Press; ©Rudy Umans/Shutterstock; ©JupiterImages *(bottom row, left to right)* ©JupiterImages; ©Cambridge University Press; ©Danilo Calilung/Corbis   **56** ©Mike Powell/Getty Images   **58** *(sweater)* ©Karina Bakalyan/Shutterstock; *(skirt)* ©Ruslan Kudrin/Shutterstock; *(jeans)* ©Karkas/Shutterstock *(all others)* ©Cambridge University Press   **60** ©George Kerrigan   **64** *(clockwise from top left)* ©Belinda Images/SuperStock; ©Ingram Publishing/SuperStock; ©Blend Images/SuperStock; ©Punchstock *(mouse)* ©urfin/Shutterstock   **66** *(top row, left to right)* ©Catherine Karnow/Corbis; ©Shawn Baldwin/EPA/Newscom; ©Fotosonline/Alamy *(middle row, left to right)* ©Peter Willi/SuperStock; ©Douglas Pulsipher/Alamy; ©KSTFoto/Alamy *(bottom row, left to right)* ©Cambridge University Press; ©Prisma Bildagentur AG/Alamy; ©S.T. Yiap Still Life/Alamy   **67** *(top to bottom)* ©Bob Krist/Corbis; ©Ron Erwin/Getty Images; ©Bert Hoferichter/Alamy   **68** *(clockwise from top left)* ©Enzo/agefotostock; ©Olga Lyubkina/Shutterstock; ©Olga Miltsova/Shutterstock; ©Joseph Dilag/Shutterstock   **69** ©Steve Hix/Somos Images/Corbis   **71** *(top to bottom)* ©Laura Coles/Getty Images; ©Datacraft Co Ltd/Getty Images; ©panda3800/Shutterstock   **72** *(top to bottom)* ©Stephen Johnson/Getty Images; ©Simon DesRochers/Masterfile; ©ImagesEurope/Alamy; ©David Robinson/Snap2000 Images/Alamy75 © Best View Stock/Alamy   **76** ©Thinkstock   **82** ©Thinkstock   **84** *(top to bottom)* ©Exactostock/SuperStock; ©Joe McBride/Getty Images   **85** ©David Young-Wolff/PhotoEdit   **87** ©Blend Images/SuperStock   **90** *(clockwise from top left)* ©Cambridge University Press; ©Alexander Raths/Shutterstock; ©Cambridge University Press; ©Africa Studio/Shutterstock; ©Cambridge University Press; ©Cambridge University Press; ©Cambridge University Press; ©Cambridge University Press; ©Lepas/Shutterstock; ©Luis Carlos Jimenez del rio/Shutterstock; ©Jonelle Weaver/Getty Images; ©Cambridge University Press; ©Tetra Images/SuperStock; ©Cambridge University Press; ©Nixx Photography/Shutterstock; ©Orange Stock Photo Production Inc./Alamy; ©simpleman/Shutterstock   **91** ©jet/Shutterstock   **92** *(top row, left to right)* ©Cambridge University Press; ©Cambridge University Press; ©Cambridge University Press; ©Thinkstock; ©Cambridge University Press *(top middle row, left to right)* ©Ryan McVay/Thinkstock; ©Valentyn Volkov/Shutterstock; ©Thinkstock; ©Cambridge University Press; ©Cambridge University Press *(bottom middle row, left to right)* ©Cambridge University Press; ©Cambridge University Press; ©Cambridge University Press; ©Cambridge University Press; ©Multiart/Shutterstock *(bottom row, left to right)* ©Cambridge University Press; ©Cambridge University Press; ©Cambridge University Press; ©Cambridge University Press; ©svry/Shutterstock   **93** *(top to bottom)* ©Cambridge University Press; ©Thinkstock; ©Thinkstock; ©Fuse/Getty Images/RF   **96** ©Lena Pantiukh/Shutterstock

Text credits

While every effort has been made, it has not always been possible to identify the sources of all the material used, or to trace all copyright holders. If any omissions are brought to our notice, we will be happy to include the appropriate acknowledgements on reprinting.

Special thanks to Kerry S. Vrabel for his editorial contributions.

The top 500 spoken words

This is a list of the top 500 words in spoken North American English. It is based on a sample of four and a half million words of conversation from the Cambridge International Corpus. The most frequent word, *I*, is at the top of the list.

1. I	40. really	79. see
2. and	41. with	80. how
3. the	42. he	81. they're
4. you	43. one	82. kind
5. uh	44. are	83. here
6. to	45. this	84. from
7. a	46. there	85. did
8. that	47. I'm	86. something
9. it	48. all	87. too
10. of	49. if	88. more
11. yeah	50. no	89. very
12. know	51. get	90. want
13. in	52. about	91. little
14. like	53. at	92. been
15. they	54. out	93. things
16. have	55. had	94. an
17. so	56. then	95. you're
18. was	57. because	96. said
19. but	58. go	97. there's
20. is	59. up	98. I've
21. it's	60. she	99. much
22. we	61. when	100. where
23. huh	62. them	101. two
24. just	63. can	102. thing
25. oh	64. would	103. her
26. do	65. as	104. didn't
27. don't	66. me	105. other
28. that's	67. mean	106. say
29. well	68. some	107. back
30. for	69. good	108. could
31. what	70. got	109. their
32. on	71. OK	110. our
33. think	72. people	111. guess
34. right	73. now	112. yes
35. not	74. going	113. way
36. um	75. were	114. has
37. or	76. lot	115. down
38. my	77. your	116. we're
39. be	78. time	117. any

The top 500 spoken words

118. he's	161. five	204. sort
119. work	162. always	205. great
120. take	163. school	206. bad
121. even	164. look	207. we've
122. those	165. still	208. another
123. over	166. around	209. car
124. probably	167. anything	210. true
125. him	168. kids	211. whole
126. who	169. first	212. whatever
127. put	170. does	213. twenty
128. years	171. need	214. after
129. sure	172. us	215. ever
130. can't	173. should	216. find
131. pretty	174. talking	217. care
132. gonna	175. last	218. better
133. stuff	176. thought	219. hard
134. come	177. doesn't	220. haven't
135. these	178. different	221. trying
136. by	179. money	222. give
137. into	180. long	223. I'd
138. went	181. used	224. problem
139. make	182. getting	225. else
140. than	183. same	226. remember
141. year	184. four	227. might
142. three	185. every	228. again
143. which	186. new	229. pay
144. home	187. everything	230. try
145. will	188. many	231. place
146. nice	189. before	232. part
147. never	190. though	233. let
148. only	191. most	234. keep
149. his	192. tell	235. children
150. doing	193. being	236. anyway
151. cause	194. bit	237. came
152. off	195. house	238. six
153. I'll	196. also	239. family
154. maybe	197. use	240. wasn't
155. real	198. through	241. talk
156. why	199. feel	242. made
157. big	200. course	243. hundred
158. actually	201. what's	244. night
159. she's	202. old	245. call
160. day	203. done	246. saying

The top 500 spoken words

247. dollars	290. started	333. believe
248. live	291. job	334. thinking
249. away	292. says	335. funny
250. either	293. play	336. state
251. read	294. usually	337. until
252. having	295. wow	338. husband
253. far	296. exactly	339. idea
254. watch	297. took	340. name
255. week	298. few	341. seven
256. mhm	299. child	342. together
257. quite	300. thirty	343. each
258. enough	301. buy	344. hear
259. next	302. person	345. help
260. couple	303. working	346. nothing
261. own	304. half	347. parents
262. wouldn't	305. looking	348. room
263. ten	306. someone	349. today
264. interesting	307. coming	350. makes
265. am	308. eight	351. stay
266. sometimes	309. love	352. mom
267. bye	310. everybody	353. sounds
268. seems	311. able	354. change
269. heard	312. we'll	355. understand
270. goes	313. life	356. such
271. called	314. may	357. gone
272. point	315. both	358. system
273. ago	316. type	359. comes
274. while	317. end	360. thank
275. fact	318. least	361. show
276. once	319. told	362. thousand
277. seen	320. saw	363. left
278. wanted	321. college	364. friends
279. isn't	322. ones	365. class
280. start	323. almost	366. already
281. high	324. since	367. eat
282. somebody	325. days	368. small
283. let's	326. couldn't	369. boy
284. times	327. gets	370. paper
285. guy	328. guys	371. world
286. area	329. god	372. best
287. fun	330. country	373. water
288. they've	331. wait	374. myself
289. you've	332. yet	375. run

The top 500 spoken words

376. they'll	418. company	460. sorry
377. won't	419. friend	461. living
378. movie	420. set	462. drive
379. cool	421. minutes	463. outside
380. news	422. morning	464. bring
381. number	423. between	465. easy
382. man	424. music	466. stop
383. basically	425. close	467. percent
384. nine	426. leave	468. hand
385. enjoy	427. wife	469. gosh
386. bought	428. knew	470. top
387. whether	429. pick	471. cut
388. especially	430. important	472. computer
389. taking	431. ask	473. tried
390. sit	432. hour	474. gotten
391. book	433. deal	475. mind
392. fifty	434. mine	476. business
393. months	435. reason	477. anybody
394. women	436. credit	478. takes
395. month	437. dog	479. aren't
396. found	438. group	480. question
397. side	439. turn	481. rather
398. food	440. making	482. twelve
399. looks	441. American	483. phone
400. summer	442. weeks	484. program
401. hmm	443. certain	485. without
402. fine	444. less	486. moved
403. hey	445. must	487. gave
404. student	446. dad	488. yep
405. agree	447. during	489. case
406. mother	448. lived	490. looked
407. problems	449. forty	491. certainly
408. city	450. air	492. talked
409. second	451. government	493. beautiful
410. definitely	452. eighty	494. card
411. spend	453. wonderful	495. walk
412. happened	454. seem	496. married
413. hours	455. wrong	497. anymore
414. war	456. young	498. you'll
415. matter	457. places	499. middle
416. supposed	458. girl	500. tax
417. worked	459. happen	